99 PRAY
YOUR CHURCH NEEDS
[BUT DOESN'T KNOW IT YET]

PRAYERS FOR UNPREDICTABLE
AND UNUSUAL TIMES

CARA GILGER, EDITOR

chalice
press
Saint Louis, Missouri

An imprint of Christian Board of Publication

Cover Image: ©Lightstock

Cover Design: Elizabeth Wright

Interior Design: Connie H.C. Wang

ChalicePress.com

Print: 9780827225343
EPUB: 9780827225350
EPDF: 9780827225367

Printed in the United States of America

CONTENTS

Prayers for Community in Challenging Times

Prayers for Community Discernment

Prayers and Blessings for Community Celebrations

Prayers for Your Pastor

INTRODUCTION

The looming, Southern style pulpit elevated several feet off the ground blocked the congregation's view of the small, hard pew where the preacher sits. This made it hard for the congregation to see my face as it alternated flashing a strange mix of surprise and compassion, with an equal attempt at composure. Across the chancel standing in the lectern was our Elder for the Sunday. He was known for being a tall gentleman in a well-polished gray suit, mid-40s with two teenage daughters and a string of successful entrepreneurial endeavors. As he stood in front of the congregation clutching either side of the lectern, the sanctuary was silent as we listened to the muffled gulping sound that erupted mid-prayer and the silence that followed as he tried to compose himself amid sobs to complete his morning prayer.

The next morning, the senior pastor, who had been out of town, came by my office to see how my solo weekend preaching and leading worship had gone, as this was my first as a seminary student at the church.

"I heard it went well," he began in his usual exuberant way, "You took my advice on your sermon."

I nodded in agreement, even though I had not and paused mulling over what to say next. "Did you already hear about the prayer?" I asked. He looked at me blankly and shook his head so I continued, "Well, the Elder who was doing the morning prayer, he went to Virginia Tech...did anyone on staff know that?" I paused, "He tried to pray for his alma mater, but instead he broke down crying..."

This had all taken place on Sunday, April 22, 2007, the first Sunday after a mass shooting took place on the campus of Virginia Tech.

The Elder in my church wanted to say something meaningful. He had wanted to say a word on behalf of the people gathered in worship to a loving and present God. He had wanted to say something about suffering and heartache, about brokenness and hope. He wanted a prayer that connected to people who were grieving, and he wanted to do something to connect his own heartache with God's embrace. But sometimes in the midst of the rawness of an event or the closeness of heartache or even the intensity of celebration, it is hard to find the words to articulate our deeply human sorrows, longing and joy to God in community.

The conventional wisdom goes, "You don't know what you don't know," and when it comes to ministry—this beautiful, creative, and messy thing God does when people gather and try to build honest, authentic, and loving community—this is certainly true. I remember my first year of ministry slipping into my office, closing the door quietly so as not to alert my suitemates, and calling my closest friend in ministry. In a hushed tone, I remember confessing what I didn't know, and what had caught me off guard, and wondering aloud if today was the day everyone would find out I secretly didn't know what I was doing.

Sometimes we just don't know what we don't know. We don't know our days will be spent breaking up arguments between volunteers at the church garage sale, or that our evenings will be filled with tense leadership meetings about church finances, or that members of our beloved community would face unspeakable personal circumstances and invite us to join them in those tender, sacred moments. And we may not know how to meet them in these moments with the fullness of God's holy presence.

There's a technical term for this—it's called imposters syndrome. After years as a pastor of spiritual formation, I am aware that when it comes to prayer, often the leaders we serve alongside have a sense that they are woefully inadequate to the task of prayer, at least in the public form it takes when we gather in Christian community. Whether around board meeting tables or personnel gathering or worship, often in the face of new or challenging moments, we find our words inadequate to the size of the situation in which God meets us.

It is in the spirit of these moments that 99 Prayers was imagined. Sometimes you don't know what obstacles you might face as a minister or church leader, but you may have the sense that prayer is needed in challenging, transitional, and discerning moments. You may know that the Spirit of God that is always present needs space cleared through the practice of prayer to inhabit our moments of need and joy.

At the heart of prayer is a deep longing to connect our lives to the heart of God, but as Henri Nouwen explains, "Prayer is not something that comes naturally or easily. It is something that requires learning and discipline." 99 Prayers is a tool for learning how to pray together in unexpected circumstances and a companion for when you know you *need* to pray, but you are not sure *what* to pray.

Enclosed in this book you will find prayers for unexpected circumstance from the deeply troubling to the truly celebratory and those times in between. Created to be a resource for pastors and leaders as a reference and guide, they are a starting place for imagining how one might pray in unexpected moments. These prayers are not meant to be the exact perfect prayer for your specific ministry context, rather, they are a suggested starting point for reflecting on where God is and how God might meet us in a particular moment. Perhaps a sentence or two or a turn of phrase will catch your spiritual imagination and set you on the path to writing a prayer that fits you and your situation authentically.

In the end, our prayers in difficult times are much less about having the right words, as they are about having the right spirit. They are about a spirit of genuine care for the people and community you hold dear.

The prayers included in these pages were written by clergy serving in a variety of ministry contexts across the country. The authors each reflect the diversity of these contexts as well as the diverse theologies represented within Bethany Fellowships.

Prayers for Individuals in Challenging Times

A family in your congregation has experienced a traumatic death

God, we cry out to you today confused, hurting, and not prepared for this moment. But here and now we turn to you, and to each other, seeking strength for what lies ahead.

We thank you for the gift of (insert deceased name), and we hold tight to (her/his/their) presence, which we sense is still close.

Guide this family, O God, and allow them to accept help from those who love them. When they feel lost or afraid, comfort them with your presence, and with the knowledge that they are being held by a greater and deeper love, O God. May your love, which will be made known in family and friends, be steadfast and near in the days ahead.

In the Name of the Living Christ we pray. Amen.

A member of your congregation has committed suicide

God of strength, we come to you in these moments of deep hurt and confusion. Wrap our souls with your unconditional love to hold our broken hearts, seeking understanding of how a person would feel so alone to take their own life. We feel struggle as we wish we had seen signs that would have helped (deceased name).

Receive (deceased name) in your divine care like no other presence could. In the absence of works may we simply hold this dear one to you in your unfailing light so as to shine a presence of companionship that seemed missing in their life. Let us lean into your presence as our own faith is shaken. We turn to you as our rock and foundation during this time of struggle and pain. May Christ, who knew pain, guide us in the days to come. We pray in your holy name. Amen.

For those who have lost a loved one to an overdose

God of eternal presence, we stand in the unsettled stillness of uninvited grief. We confess our powerlessness over the wretchedness of drug addiction. We, who have stood upon the precipice of lost hope, who have prayed our desperate hearts dry, who have burned with frustrated anger among the broken pieces of shattered promises, stand now before you in exhausted lament.

We call upon your merciful hand to touch the tender wounds of betrayal, that deep well of sadness, and heal us. We ask that you release us from the remaining power of addiction that survives the death of our beloved (deceased name). We ask for grace to endure the misunderstanding of others and deliverance from the clouds of shame. We yearn for your light and recovery of wholeness for we who hold the memory of your beloved in our hearts. It is in the Spirit of the resurrected Christ we pray. Amen.

A member or close relative of the congregation passes away on deployment

O God, my Lord,
Keeper of my heart and guardian of my soul,
Reach me through the darkness of this moment.
I am empty.
I am alone.
I am surrounded by a war a thousand miles away;
And I feel lost in its noise and destruction even here.
Hear my plea, God, for my heart is broken:
A good friend and saint of my beloved church was killed in
    action.
In my own mind I strived to prepare my heart for this
    possibility,
"You've buried saints before this and you will bury saints after
    this,"
But this grief is different;
It is filled with a discriminate anger: at the enemy, at the
    military, at my country.
These perpetual wars continue to manipulate my deepest
    being.
I am a tear-stained servant; I try to heal myself of this loss.
I search for the familiar words of assurance; I cannot find them.
I wrestle with how I will speak love to the casualties of this
    moment,
Her father, her mother, her brothers, her friends - all that
    prayed to you for her.
Sometimes I wonder, God, whether war creates more tears
    than you can hold in your heart,
But I pray you hold my friend within your peace.
Hear my prayer, O God, my Lord. Amen.

A member of your community is facing mental health issues

Creator God, you made humanity in your image and said that it was very good. You knit us together in our mother's womb, and we are fearfully and wonderfully made. But sometimes darkness casts a shadow on the beauty of your creation; a darkness that overwhelms and suffocates; a darkness found in the wilderness of mental illness.

We blame those who suffer, calling them weak, crazy, and broken, but it's not their fault. This disease of the mind is debilitating, life altering, and dangerous. For the afflicted, there are no feelings of peace and no reassurance of comfort, and little hope remains. Fear has replaced control.

Provide us with the tools to care for our friends and neighbors. Encourage us to educate ourselves, not only so we can spread awareness, but so we can also cultivate compassion and promote better understanding.

For those who suffer, we pray for peace. For those wandering in the wilderness, we pray for a glimpse of paradise. For those trying so hard to get back to what used to be, we pray for acceptance of the new normal that is to come.

God of comfort, we know that you are in control even when our mind tells us otherwise. You are there for your children who are hurting and scared. You reach down with your loving hand and calm the storm that rages within. It is to you, O God, that we look for our guidance and hope as we pray in the name of Jesus Christ. Amen.

A member of your congregation is struggling with depression

God you know how dark the darkness can be, and you know how much pain the human heart can hold. (Name) is suffering right now, this disease of depression has reared up one more time and it is telling (her/him/them) lies about who they are and who you created them to be in your image, O God. Depression tells us that we are nothing, that the world is empty, that we are alone. But God we pray: come now and be the truth, come and be the morning that follows the night of weeping. Come, God, and speak your promises again; come and be hope; come and be the strength and courage for another minute, another hour, another day. Surround (name) with your loving care; send them the help and company they need, and make your presence known to them in these difficult days, bringing them rest and peace. Amen.

A member in your congregation is experiencing personal financial crisis

Holy One,
At times we feel so far from your radical abundance,
far from having what we need to flourish and to thrive,
far from a financial space of stability and safety.
Your people are no stranger to these wilderness times-
as the Israelites longed for the promised land,
as Abraham waited for a people,
as Sarah yearned for a child,
so we desire a space of security, a place where we have access
    to the resources we need.
We are not alone in this seeking, in this desiring, in this
    yearning for peace of mind.
Your people have walked this road before, and you have walked
    with them.
Step by step, day by day,
and today, Holy One, you walk with us still.
Strengthen us for the work ahead.
Embolden us to seek out resources, services, and the assistance
    we require,
Remind us that to yearn for something better,
for flourishing and abundance, for stability and security,
requires courage, persistence, and faithfulness, and all of this
    is indeed possible because we are not alone.
As you have been with your people throughout history,
so you are with us now, as
step by step, day by day,
you walk with us still.
Thanks be to God.
Amen.

A member is placing their spouse into assisted living

God of all our days,

God who holds the future: Sometimes it is so hard to change. We come into different seasons of life; we are faced with new challenges as well as new limitations; and sometimes we must make impossible choices. We lift up to you our sister/brother (name) who has had to make one of those choices. God, we pray now that you will give (him/her/them) peace, that you will protect them from doubt, fear, and guilt, and that you will walk beside them through this time of change.

And we pray also for (spouse's name), that you will be present to (her/him/them), that you will speak to their heart and help them believe that they are safe and loved. Faithful God, as you have been in this marriage always, continue to be part of it now, and show the way into the future. Amen.

A member of your congregation has miscarried

God of the brokenhearted,

We come to you this day with sighs too deep for words. We hold the (insert name) family in your light. God, they were expecting a child, not this pain. They were expecting sleepless nights with a crying infant, not sleepless nights filled with the utter despair of silence. They were expecting the cries of a newborn, and instead they are holding the cries of their own grief. Comfort them, O God.

Lay your healing presence upon broken hearts. And God, we pray that you embolden us to surround them in our prayers and our love both in word and in deed. Help us to hold their grief tenderly with them, reminding them that they are not alone. Reminding them that just as you surround them with loving care, O God, so does this community of faith. May we together lean into you as we seek your healing and your hope. Amen.

Social services has become involved with a family in your community

O God,
You seek to shelter us all as a mother hen, pulling us into the safety of your embrace.
And yet sometimes we do not experience that safety in our relationships.
As flawed and sinful human beings,
We can fall short of caring for one another.
We can experience pain caused by those who are called to love us.
In this time of unknowing, in this time of questions, anger, and distress,
O God we come to you.
Where there is need for reconciliation and open hearts and minds.
Where there is need for protection, shelter your children from harm.
Where there is hate and anger, be a source of peace.
Grant all involved your wisdom and mercy.
Guide us in the pursuit of justice and safety for all your beloved children.
Guide us into the safety of your embrace.
Amen.

For someone beginning treatment for a longterm illness

Great God, you are our refuge and strength, our very present help in times of trouble. We turn to you now, lifting (name) in love and care. Enfold (her/him/them) in your protective embrace. Hold their heart within your heart and make your abiding presence known during each and every step of the journey that lies ahead. Reside with them as they sit in waiting rooms and exam rooms. Provide them with courageous fortitude during all tests, procedures, and treatments. Grant them your peace, especially during times of anxious waiting and uncertainty. Gift the entire care team with wisdom, compassion, and the expertise needed to provide the best care to our beloved. (name) is your precious child, your beautiful creation. Embolden and empower them now—in mind, body, and spirit—and instill within him/her a hopeful reassurance of your faithful promises.

Bring your wholeness to brokenness, your healing to illness, your strength to weakness, and cover us in your all-surpassing grace. We trust in your healing Spirit and providential care. Amen.

A family in your church is being deported unexpectedly

O God, Dieu, Dios, and Gott, (inserting any other language within the community) we are a community from many different backgrounds, cultures, and journeys, but we are all gathered here, following your call to love and support one another. Be with the (insert name) family, as your beloved children face the challenge of staying in the land they call home. May they know that you are with them on every step of the journey. Help them to know that they are yours without reservations or papers. And may we as a community help them to know your church is built on people and not boundaries. This is not a struggle they face alone.

Holy One, be with each of us as we offer sanctuary in our hearts when we cannot offer the security of space. We follow Jesus, as one born in persecution, forced to leave home and family behind, and yet returned into your loving embrace. May we act with such courage and faith, and forever keep in our hearts your abundant love and eternal grace. In the name of Jesus the Christ, we pray. Amen.

PRAYERS AND BLESSINGS
FOR INDIVIDUALS

Blessing for a church member who is starting a new job

Like the first sip of coffee in the morning,
May this new beginning fill you with joyful anticipation.
May you feel possibilities rising up inside you,
Opportunities to use your gifts in fresh ways,
To offer yourself to each day with energy and excitement.
I pray that you look forward to the start of each day's work,
Knowing that you hold within you all you need to meet its
     challenges,
That your particular blend of wisdom, creativity, and vision
Is enough to satisfy whatever this day asks of you.
Breathe in the beautiful aroma of this vocation,
And be filled with confidence that God has called you to this
     work.
Let the warmth of the Spirit flow through you,
Awakening your unique mix of experiences, hopes, dreams,
     and questions.
Speaking love through your words and actions,
Fueling your passions and compassion for the tasks in front of
     you each day.
Amen.

A member of your congregation is celebrating a milestone in sobriety

God of joyful hope, we come before you with profound humility and gratitude for your daily grace. We marvel in your faithfulness and your capacity and desire to turn our shame into peace. We trust in your goodness to lead us by your light and feed us by your Word. Thank you for the gift of sobriety. Thank you for the healing of relationships and the hope of healing where it has not yet occurred.

Give us strength in our surrender, peace in our powerlessness, happiness in our humility. May we extend our hand to those beside and behind us. Transform us into exemplars and open channels of your will and your amazing grace. Withhold from us not the joy of passing along to the afflicted and their families the freedom that was so freely given to us. Let us be witnesses to the power to live in the light of your love one day at a time.

It is to a God whom we seek to understand and know day by day that we offer this prayer. Amen.

Blessing for a family who is making a long-distance move

Holy one, we gather into your presence to lift up by name the (name) family as they prepare their hearts and home for a move from this community to a community that they do not know. O God, you traveled with the Israelites from Egypt to the Promise Land, you traveled with Ruth and Naomi to Moab, and you traveled with Mary and Joseph to Bethlehem and on to Egypt with the infant Jesus, because you are a God that goes with us.

Comfort them as they leave what is familiar to them in this place and embolden them to build the life you envision for them in their new home. As we anticipate the relocation of (name) family, we pray that you would make your presence closely known to them.

We pray that you, O God, would be with them, making their transition smooth and filled with unexpected joys. Bless the (name) family as we pray this in the name of the one who comforts and guides your people, Jesus Christ. Amen.

For the new identity of one who is transitioning

Gracious God, we give thanks for (insert name), whom you have called by name and made yours. Through the struggle for authentic and holy identity, you were there. Through the rough waters of challenges to wholeness, you were there. Through the fires that destroyed what was and purified what will be, you were there. And here, too, you are, calling forth what is new, what is holy, what is true in (name).

We give you thanks and praise for your faithfulness, your loving kindness, your patient grace as you call into being this full creation in your image; this transformed one in your love. And we ask your blessing on (name), on the beloved community surrounding (her/him/them), and on this world that today is called again to love, support, and celebrate (name).

Unleash your Spirit on (her/him/them) so that (her/him/them) may know most fully that your love has never left them and resides in them now and always. In Jesus Christ, the transformed one who transforms us all, we pray. Amen.

For those who serve behind the scenes in ministry

Remembering that you, Christ, came not to be served, but to serve humbly,

We give thanks today for those quiet and humble servants among us

They do not ask for praise, yet their quiet diligence helps us to praise you.

Because of them, our cups overflow with coffee, communion juice, and grace.

Our worship spaces are emptied of discarded bulletins and displaced pride.

In quiet and often imperceptible ways, they teach us what it means to love like you:

Not for any reward or glory, but for the pure joy of offering yourself for the good of all.

Bless these often-unnoticed disciples of the kitchen and classroom, the copy room, and garden.

We celebrate their contributions to this community,

Knowing that without them the body of Christ would not function as a complete and meaningful whole.

With gratitude we offer this prayer to you, the servant of all. Amen.

Blessing for students who are leaving to study abroad

God of all times and place,

We celebrate that you have called students from our community to be sent out into the world to learn, to listen, and to engage. In the path of countless others, they have been sent to a new place – on a pilgrimage of sorts – away from home, to discover the home they carry with them wherever they go—the home they find in you.

We pray for (insert name/names) who is journeying to (destination).

God, we ask for your abundant presence with (this/these) students. When they feel lonely, may they know you are with them. When they see something new, may they know that you make all things new. When they are afraid, may they know your wisdom that repeats, "fear not." When they learn something new, may their minds be open. When they wander, may they make discoveries off the beaten path. Give them enough companionship on this adventure to sustain them and enough longing to keep them open to new people. Give them enough comfort to care for themselves and enough discomfort for them to not take anything for granted. Give them curiosity to ask questions and give them enough answers to keep the questions coming.

We thank you for the students—for the impact this adventure will have on them and the ways you will use that into their and our shared future. Amen.

A member of your congregation is formally changing their name (refugees)

Read Isaiah 62:2b-4a
> You will be called by a new name
>> that the mouth of the LORD will bestow.
> You will be a crown of splendor in the LORD's hand,
>> a royal diadem in the hand of your God.
> No longer will they call you Deserted,
>> or name your land Desolate.
> But you will be called Hephzibah,
>> and your land Beulah;
>> for the LORD will take delight in you. (NIV)

Leader: Dear sister/brother, you will now be called by a new name, that the Lord will bestow.

For the Lord delights in you. You will be known as the child of God you are, fearfully and wonderfully made.

(Make cross with water on individual's forehead, recalling both baptism and anointing)

Leader: We give thanks to you, God, for your servant (name). May his/her name be written on your heart.

All: May our God, who knows your name, bless you and guide you.

A family in your congregation is welcoming a foster child

God, we delight with (insert parent and other children's names) as they receive a new child into their family, and we look forward with joy to getting to know (name of foster child). For the days, months, or years this child is a part of our community, help us to embrace (her/him/them).

We give thanks, O God, that you so graciously open your arms to all children. Open our hearts to extend love and grace to this child; to share with them the stories of our faith; to be challenged by them and to grow in faith with them; to treasure this time together; and to support (parents' name) in nurturing this child of theirs, ours, and yours. And, if we must one day say goodbye, grant us the strength to release (name of child) into your care and to remain in prayer for them. In Jesus' name we pray. Amen

A prayer with a child for the passing of their pet

God of all creation, everything you created and formed was good. We are so thankful for the animals that become special to us and become a part of our home and family. Each pet that we have has a special place in our hearts. We say this prayer today for a special pet named (name of the pet) and for the meaningful way this member of the family brought joy and love to all in this household. We give thanks for the days of care, play, and love that have been shared with (name of the pet). We will continue to hold a place in our hearts to always remember how this gift of yours has been a gift to us. We share this prayer in the name of the one who blesses all creatures of our world. Amen.

PRAYERS FOR COMMUNITY IN CHALLENGING TIMES

A medical emergency occurs
during worship

Holy God, hear us, calm us, gather us into your Spirit's peace. We shake in need of grace, and for fear of (insert name), whose sudden emergency calls us to call out to you.

Your healing ways remain mysterious. We don't know exactly what to expect when we cry for help, but we trust you are present, and listen and love us.

So, receive our desperate, pleading words that whatever wholeness is possible be restored to our beloved sister/ brother. God, we pray that those are continuing to assist do so with calm, clarity, and skill. Receive our gratitude, too, that people reacted with compassion.

As we continue in worship, make our hearts hopeful of abundant life for all, but most especially for (name), your child, whom we're glad to count among our own. This we pray, in the name of the One who makes us one forever. Amen.

Your congregation is struggling to pay bills

God our provider,
You are faithful in mercy and you are abundant in grace.
We confess to you our fear of financial failure.
Our anxiety in the face of obligations,
Our uncertainty about tomorrow,
Our grief over the loss of yesterday's security,
Have found us in the wilderness of desperation.
With humility and thanksgiving we ask this blessing:
We ask that you would dissolve the shadows of fear hanging
    over your people, O Lord,
Which distort our perception,
Which obscure creative solutions,
Which tempt us to believe the lies of scarcity.
Restore our faith in your provision.
Grant us the courage to make difficult decisions.
Console our troubled hearts.
Breathe in us the spirit of expectation for the new thing you
    are about to do.
We pray to you these things with the resurrection hope of your
    beloved Son, Jesus Christ. Amen.

Your building has been on fire

Loving God, we come seeking answers to give us peace of mind. This is something that we are definitely not accustomed to. The fire that has touched the foundations of our church this times one which forces us to reassess how we are to do worship, until we recover from such a tragedy. We are not used to experiencing fire in this manner. We are accustomed to experiencing the fire of the Holy Spirit fill our worship space Sunday after Sunday. This is a fire that we have often welcomed with open arms and anticipation. However, this time, a physical fire has come, and our spirits yearn for the day when we can look forward to gathering in this space again. Until then, we will continue gathering as a community of faith in a different space, still meeting the needs of those around us, still meeting people where they are, still keeping the table open to those who are seeking to experience Jesus, and still anxiously waiting for the fire of the Holy Spirit to come and feel us with an unspeakable joy. Knowing that in all that we have lost, through you, we are able to recover that and more. And for that we are grateful. Therefore, we say thank you! In Jesus' name we pray. Amen!

Your building's sprinkler system goes off and damages your church property

We give thanks, O God, that the damage was limited and that fire was restricted. We celebrate that the people we are called to serve through the instrument of this building are safe. O God, give us clear heads and focused vision to restore our building, so that we might restore our missional tool in this community. Invite us to be faithful in discerning of next steps, responsible in managing repairs, and engage our sense of gratitude and holy humor as we move through this opportunity to continue our faithful service in Christ Jesus. Amen.

Your church has been burglarized

God who calls us and cares for us.

Today we offer you all that we are feeling. Our anger. Our fear. Our confusion. Our grief.

We know this place to be holy as we experience your presence here and with one another. We do not understand how one of your children could or would steal from and damage this place, this community. Comfort us, O God. Give us strength to let go of what has been lost as we remember that our trust is only in you. Give us grace to process what has happened. And, God, give us the courage to live the prayer of Jesus as we "forgive those who sin against us."

We pray for those who committed this crime, that they would change the path they are on and to know, regardless of their actions, that they too are your beloved. Guide us forward as we clean up, assess the damage, and do the work of compassion in ourselves and in our world. Amen.

Your church has been vandalized

God, we come before you wondering. Why would someone tear down rather than build up? How could this happen in a space we hold as sacred and safe? Who would do this? We don't understand, and yet we know you are present with us in the pain and a light within us despite our confusion. You, for whom darkness is light, who call us out to be a people of light; you stand in all places of disorientation, destruction, and pain. Help us not to lose trust in others, but to seek out ways to grow our resilience through you. Guide us as we find ways to be a people of light in a world that needs us. Give us courage to continue to live boldly in this place knowing the faith, love, and trust you place in us to be your people. We know you call us to stand with others just as you stand with us. Help us to continue to offer hospitality with our building and our lives even though we are sometimes hurt and betrayed. Allow us the passion and compassion to continue to be a people of your love in this place. In Jesus Christ's name, Amen.

Your community has sustained a significant disaster

Holy Creator, we come before you dazed, tired, and overwhelmed by the significant disaster that has happened in our community. The news, our insurance, they use the words "act of God" to describe what has happened to our community, but we know that you did not cause (insert specific disaster, (for example,: tornado, flood, fire, earthquake), but nevertheless have met us in this moment. Be present with us, O God, in our grief and sense of loss, not just of possessions and routines, but of a sense of security. We have an increased knowledge of the wildness of this world. Comfort us, O God, in our fear and our trauma.

Create in us a sense of security in your presence, O God. Through the manifestation of your loving care made known through the loving care of this community and how we care for one another in this time and place, may we see the love of Christ Jesus and the presence of the Holy Spirit. Allow us the privilege of showing your love through the way we serve our community in this time of deep need and grief, O God. As we clean up the wreckage caused by this disaster, let us see the potential of new life you are creating and let us meet it creatively and joyfully. We pray all of this in the name of the one whom you sent to meet us in the messy chaos of our lives and of this world, Jesus the Christ. Amen.

Your community has sustained a significant economic disaster

God of Bankruptcy, Foreclosure, and Insolvency, *or*

God of Market Corrections, Recessions, and Depressions, *or* God of the Laborers and the Unions, *or* God of the Executives and the Board Rooms, *or*

God of Abundance and God of Scarcity,

As we watch our storehouses of trust and financial well-being suddenly swept bare, we struggle to find the right words. We stand in anxiety and worry at what will happen now that:

our national economy has broken again under the weight of our overconsumption and greed, *or*

the local plant has announced its plans to close and layoff its workforce, *or*

our state tax policy has left the weakest and poorest among us with no safety net, no education, and no basic quality of life, *or* one of our church employees has taken advantage of our trust and stolen communal resources for their personal use.

Find our church in our fear of a future we cannot yet imagine, and hold us close to you, Rock of Ages. Embrace us tightly in your arms of security, wholeness, and courage. When the opportunities arise for us to seek our common welfare, give us voice to speak our truth for ourselves and for those who will lose the most in these days. In our own loss, live with us in disease and love us in our discomfort.

Occupy our hearts with your peace, and move through us to seek clarity, mercy, restoration, and justice as this crisis rewrites our community's story. Amen.

Your congregation experiences a significant drop in membership

Through every valley you lead us, O God, through *every* season. So, in this time of goodbyes, you lead us still. Thank you.

Yet we stand before you feeling diminished, through the loss not merely of church members, but of ministries, friendships, and future possibilities. Help us abide our hurt with grace and not bitterness, with confidence and not criticism, with hope and not defeat.

And hear our prayers for those we've lost, that they find loving communities that feed and challenge them.

And for ourselves, that our eyes open to fresh opportunities, our hearts to new dreams, our hands to friendships not yet known, but expected in faith. While we grieve the loss of beloved members of this community, allow us to hold space in our hearts for people you have yet to send to this place.

God of the valleys and hilltops, we worship you, content with our place in your reign of unconditional love, followers always of the *resurrected* son, by whom we pray. Amen.

Your congregation has sustained the passing of a member

God of All,

Today we cry out to you at the loss of one among us. Some of us are in shock. Some of us are angry. Some of us feel nothing as we cannot believe this to be true.

Hear our cries, O God. As we hear the cries of the family, support us as we support them. Be patient with us and grant us patience to walk the long road of healing with those closest to the one whom we grieve.

Guide us to lean toward one another and toward you. We cannot picture our church without him/her. It feels as though our community is broken from the inside out. The harsh reality is that we will never be the same, and yet even this pain continues your story of love, pain, healing, and hope. On that holy Saturday, the day after Jesus died, the disciples sat in their despair not knowing what or how they could go on, and yet new life was awaiting them. It did not diminish the pain, but it offered hope for healing. We are a people of hope. (Insert deceased's name) was a person of hope. O God help us to know that death is never the end of the story for (Name) or for our community. We give you thanks for (Name's) life and for the way he/she impacted us all. As we grieve together, may we be made anew. Amen.

Your congregation is about to implement a staff reduction

God who knows all our joys and all our anxieties, all our gifts and all our fears, today we seek the assurance of your life-giving presence and guidance in the life of the church. As we implement a reduction in staff, may your wisdom direct our discourse and compassion fill our actions. These changes are sad and painful, and we especially pray that you would tend to the staff person(s) whose position is eliminated. We long for their well-being and ache for the difficult situation in which we put them. Have mercy on them and on us. Grant that we would experience abundance where now we see only scarcity for we know you are a God of life. We turn to you also on behalf of the staff who will remain, that they would be granted renewed energy even in the face of loss and transition. Empower us, as a congregation to support our staff and aid us in our collaboration with one another. Amen.

Your congregation is letting go of a staff member

Oh God, in the life of discipleship, we want everything to work. We want people to be fed, inspired, and cared for. We want kindness and compassion to rule in our hearts, and spread from us like a beacon of hope to all who see us.

But alas, we are human beings. We make mistakes. We want to forgive, and be gracious, but sometimes those mistakes mean things need to change.

Hold our frustration, our disappointment, our anger. Hold our fears and resentments, our questions that can't be answered. Restore to us, Holy One, our faith that you are our purpose, and yours is our mission. Help us find your likeness in each other again, that we may trust those who had to make this difficult decision, and cover our hurt with love.

In Christ we worship. in Christ we serve, and in Christ we pray. Amen.

Your congregation is being protested

(The bolded words are a communal response; the non-bolded words may be read by a single leader, or numerous leaders, may also be adapted to be read in a single part)

Holy and Loving God of all peoples, places and philosophies, we gather together in community seeking sanctuary.

May our voices proclaim your faithfulness always.

Incline your ear to us over the din of others, amplify your Word in our hearts, breathe into us new life through your Spirit.

You have called us to be agents of reconciliation, workers in the harvest of justice, and lovers of mercy.

Just as you love us individually and as a congregation,

You so love the world, too.

We ask your blessing, Holy and Loving God, on those outside of this sanctuary today.

We ask your blessing on those that protest this congregation and the work we do in the Reign of God.

We ask you to protect and strengthen these protestors,

May their bodies be kept whole, safe, and secure while they are in our presence.

We ask that you bless their lives and guide their work.

May their understanding of you grow, and may their relationships reflect it.

(Continued)

We ask that your Spirit move among them,

Just as we seek your Spirit moving among us.

There is division in this world. We seek sanctuary in this moment from it.

You call us to unity, and you call us out from the security of people we already love.

Give us the strength to love the other, even if we are not loved by them yet.

Help us accept the challenge to love our enemies, and to do so for the sake of the good news of Jesus Christ.

You love us, Holy God, as individuals and as a congregation.

You so love the world, and all of those in it, as well. Amen.

Your congregation is facing a budget shortfall

Holy Sustainer, we gather to face the disheartening news that our budget is not sustainable, that our needs for ministry and our people's faithful generosity need to be aligned in a new and creative way. O God, do not allow our story—your story of your presence in this place—be shaded with pessimism and hopelessness. God, forgive us when we are tempted to slip into a narrative of scarcity—for you are a God of abundance and creation.

Remind us that you are a God that is constantly inviting us into relationship with you. Let us see this moment as an invitation to imagine our ministries anew. Join us in this work, guide us in our conversations around our resources and call us into a fuller and broader understanding of what abundant resources you have placed in our community. Amen.

Your congregation is facing a challenge with government

Holy One who is bigger than all our fears and dwells within each spark of hope, we come to you today as a community in need. We have come to the crossroads of what is legal and what is right. But we are followers of your command that, "Anyone, then, who knows the right thing to do and fails to do it, commits sin," and we are a community who aims to sin as little as possible.

We know that doing the right thing is not always easy, but we are not alone in work. Lord, guide our steps to justice, hold us steadfast in your loving embrace, and hold our challenges both present and future in your divine light. God, help us to peacefully hear and be heard by those in power, and may righteousness and peace lead those making policy so that all of creation is represented and embraced. For we are a community of your people following your holy leadership of love and justice. In Jesus' name we pray. Amen.

(*scripture from James 4:17 NRSV)

Your congregation is facing negative media coverage

Holy God, creator of the beginning and the end, we bring our full stories to you today. Lord, in this day of hyperconnectivity, a part of our story is often confused and conflated into the whole thing. Today our community grieves a part of our story that isn't being told. We feel betrayed and helpless as we are lacking control of our own narrative. But Lord, we know you have the whole story. We feel seen in your love and embraced by your omnipotence. Help us to be still and know that you are a God of the full story. May you write on the hearts of those who have not heard our part, and may you open our hearts to hear the stories of others that we do not know. May our community grow by asking the questions and not by assuming the answers. For we know we best love our neighbor by seeing you in their very creation and work, and we ask that you guide those controlling our public narrative to offer us that same vision and care. In the holy name of Jesus, we pray. Amen.

Your congregation is facing the loss of a significant community partnership

Great God! You have provided for us so many times before. When we have lacked the resources to meet our needs in the past, you made a way out of no way. Out of no way? Yes, out of no way. So, we pray this prayer without hesitation, knowing that you will come through for us now like you have done so many times before. While we grieve the loss of (community partner's name), we trust in you, God.

In a season where it seems as though we have lost much, we open our ears and eyes even more, in order to see and hear with clarity what you are calling us to now. Prepare us for what's to come. So that we may be able to rightfully adhere to this call, in this day and time, for this community that seeks to see you living through us. In Jesus' name we pray this prayer. Amen!

Your congregation is marking a first anniversary since something sad

O Holy One, we look to you now because this day weighs heavy on our bodies and souls. Admittedly, we find this past year to be remembered by distinctive change and heartbreak in our lives. You have been sustaining our world as the seasons passed and life has moved on, sometimes without us knowing. We look toward you with thanksgiving for the supporting power and comforting touch of the past year in the middle of our grief.

We join now lifting up the difficult days we've weathered. We recognize your sacred strength that helped us to continue when we didn't think we could. Now we celebrate the surprising and heartwarming moments of laughter and sparks of happiness that help us to remember the nourishment of your joyful Spirit. Help us to find by ourselves, Christ, in resurrection of change and new. We ask for you to continue to seek us even, or especially, when you feel further than you are. No matter what, let us know that your presence is all around us. Amen.

A staff member or lay leader has been discovered stealing from the church

God of Grace and Mercy, we come before you in this most difficult time, an occasion when one whom we love has violated your sacred trust. We recognize that we as a congregation are in pain and we recognize that a fellow church leader is in pain as well. The responsibility and trust that you place in each one of us to be stewards of your grace in this congregation is a gift which we do not take lightly.

In this most difficult time, empower us to be able to freely offer that grace through our forgiveness of those who have violated our trust. May your comfort and healing be upon them during this time, and may you work to restore their lives to wholeness.

Bring us your comfort and healing. Help us to acknowledge our pain and to trust that you will meet us in that place. May our congregation be restored to wholeness so that we may once again trust our leaders and empower them to serve you. All of this we pray to you. Amen.

Your organist or music leader calls in sick on Sunday

God, we pray for our music leader. We ask for your healing hand. Help them to rest, take comfort, and give them peace knowing that the Church can carry on without them. Let this congregation be a place of support and strength for them now.

What a joy it is to gather together in worship! We know that wherever two or three are gathered—Christ is there. Help us not to forget this in the rush of planning. Teach us to see this unexpected absence as an opportunity for your Spirit to move in a new way. Give our leaders a spirit of grace and laughter.

We thank you for those who may "step into" our music leader's absence this morning. Give them courage and confidence.

May all who enter these doors this morning feel the presence of your love. with us, guiding us, and strengthening us. Amen.

Your youth group experiences something frightening on mission trip

Spirit of the living God fall afresh on us, be as close as our very breath.

Spirit, we are in shock. We are scared. We don't know what to think or feel.

What we have just witnessed is not what we expected when we first set out on this journey. And yet, we know that you are still here with us. We know that you are here in the community where we are staying.

We ask that you hold us and this community in your strong and gentle arms. Surround us with your safety and your love. Spirit, give us eyes to see you in new ways as we witness this new environment. Fill us with your generosity, compassion, and love.

Open our hearts so that what breaks your heart might breaks ours as well. Open our minds so that we might learn from people, places, and experiences that are outside of our comfort zone. Open our ears that we might listen to what new things you are trying to teach us. Open our hands and guide our feet so that we might go back into the world ready to partner with our neighbors to create a world that better reflects your justice, peace, and love.

Give us strength and wisdom to stand up for your love for all people wherever we find ourselves. Amen.

A congregation member is injured at camp or on mission trip

Holy One, we are grateful for the sounds of summer: singing crickets, laughing children, and the splash of cool water. For most of us, summer is a time to play. School is out, vacations are planned, and the weather is warm. But for some of us, summer is another opportunity to answer your call in our life.

You call us to camp where we can strengthen our relationship with others while learning more about you—a place of peace and joy where your Spirit seems to flow more freely.

and/or

You call us to mission, locally and/or abroad, allowing us to share your Good News with those we meet. You give us the chance to push outside of our comfort zones while learning about your compassion.

Yet, sometimes, summertime doesn't go according to plan. Understanding that we live in a broken world, we answer your call accepting the risks that accompany your work. This means the risks of persecution and rejection alongside the risk of getting hurt, both emotionally and physically.

Today we lift up (insert name) who was injured while *at camp/ on the mission trip* knowing that your comforting arms are wrapped around (her/him/them) providing strength and healing in the days ahead. Ease their pain and surround (her/him/them) in your peace. In the name of Jesus Christ, we pray. Amen.

A member of your congregation has been discovered to be a sex offender

Dear One, we pray in the midst of our shock and confusion and grief. We can hardly take in the truth. We can hardly accept the news. We don't know what to do with ourselves or how to act toward this one who is a part of the fabric of our community. We open ourselves to your promised guidance, to Sophia wisdom, to the witness of Christ toward the outcast. We hear your call to forgiveness and to inclusion and to something else – accountability? boundaries? This day calls us to all of this and more.

So we pray for wise and knowledgeable companions to help us determine the best way forward. We pray first and foremost for ways to welcome and to protect our children in a safe, sanctuary space. We pray for the determination to welcome this one we know as friend in the midst of their chronic, not curable, addiction and illness while remaining committed to this faith community being a safe place for people to encounter God. How do we partner with them in their recovery and their best intentions and efforts to live in accountability and repentance?

We are listening in the midst of tears and hope, God. Amen.

There has been an act of extreme violence within your town or community

Why, God? Why us? Why here?
We cry out to you, God;
Our help comes
from our Rock and our Redeemer.
Do not leave us; do not forsake us.

When bodies are broken,
so too are our hearts.
When lives are torn apart,
so too is our community.
When hate tries to take hold,
so too does fear.

So, give us your love, God.

Love us even more fiercely now,
that in these moments
when life is turned upside down,
we can orient ourselves toward you.

Point us toward the helpers.
Drown out the noise of nonstop media.
Give us courage to seek comfort in community.
Remind us, again and again, that we are not alone,
and that love always wins.

Hear our prayers in whispers and shouts,
that healing would begin again,
with every Amen.

There has been an act of extreme violence perpetrated on children in your town or community

I pray, faithful God, for this community.
When innocent children are harmed, it is devastating.
Reveal your presence to us as we endure this senseless violence.
Help us, O Savior, through your power.

Hear our cry,
    for those in shock,
        comfort them, O God.
    for those who feel powerless,
        comfort them, O God.
    for those full of rage,
        comfort them, O God.
    for those blaming themselves,
        comfort them, O God.
    for those caring for victims,
        comfort them, O God.
    for those who do not yet recognize their pain,
        comfort them, O God.

Sustain us, Almighty God, through your Holy Spirit.
Our trust is in you.
Show us your unfailing love.
Rise up and provide strength as we face this unimaginable evil.
Amen.

Organization or business housed in your building has experienced public scandal

O God, who is our refuge and strength, a very present help in trouble (Psalm 46:1),

We seek your help today, O God. We seek your wisdom. We seek your peace. The Psalmist reminds us that you are our refuge, but we have come to find you, to find that refuge in this place, in our church. This building has been a refuge to our community. It is a place where we feel safe, where we are both comforted and challenged to do your work in the world.

And now, O God, we are confronted with pain that took place, here, in our sacred space. We offer to you all that we are feeling: anger, fear, sadness, confusion, and more. We do not understand how this could happen here, and yet you did not call us to be a church of isolation, but a church engaged. We cannot hide from this pain, nor should we. Embolden us to support those who are hurting. To know that in all things you are calling us toward good, toward compassion, toward love.

Help us to minister to one another, to our in-house neighbors and all impacted by this situation, not only now but long after the attention has dwindled. As we do so, O God, remind us that you are our refuge. Not a building, but you. Guide us as we do your work right here where we are. In the name of your Son, we pray. Amen.

Your community has sustained a significant social justice disaster

God of Justice, we find ourselves, our community, and our country here again.

Here again another fatal shooting of an unarmed person,
Here again another mass school shooting,
Here again a crisis that ripples from the exploitation of global lands.
Here again as creation protests the injustice of poisoned water, bodies, and global warming.

While we are here, help us to not just react but to respond by uprooting entrenched systems that perpetuate racism, classism, sexism, and heterosexism.

While we are here, help us to not go numb; give us room to hear the cries of injustice of your people.

While we are here, let us not be overwhelmed by all there is to do in the world. Help our community do something, and be something for one another, with and for the world. Amen.

A lament for racial inequality and prayer for reconciliation

God, with a somber heart, we continue to cry out to you in this climate of racial discourse. Black and Brown bodies are constantly at war with a privileged perspective that dominates our entire existence. It seems as if there is no place we can find refuge, even though we know in our hearts that you are our "Refuge and strength, a very present help in times of trouble." But when trouble tends to consume our daily walk, it is difficult to remain focused on you. Yet we strive to continue pressing forward!

We press forward with a hope that is entrenched in the belief of a loving God who sent Jesus, your son, to reconcile the chaos that we currently exist in. Through Jesus, you empowered our ancestors to fight for freedom in a land that had no desire to loosen them of their shackles and chains. And because they chose to fight for freedom until freedom was won, we will continue that same fight, until freedom is won again. Through Jesus, this was made possible before, and through Jesus, this can be made possible again. It is in that name, in Jesus' name we pray. Amen!

Your congregation is being threatened with a lawsuit

God of Justice, right now is seems like our whole world is full of uncertainty and fear. We do not know what the future will bring; we do not know if we can successfully meet the challenges before us. We are unsettled by the possibility that there are those seeking to cause us trouble. Just as you met the Israelites each new day in the wilderness, meet us in our unsettling situation.

But God, we are yours, we walk according to your will, and therefore we will not choose anger or defensiveness, we will not close our doors or our hearts, we will not turn on one another. Come what may, we will care for one another, and we will minister boldly and generously. God, guide our words, our actions, and our decisions not to the ethics of the law but to the higher ethics of your love. We pray that true justice is done; we pray that your will is done; we pray with total confidence that you will guide us through whatever happens next. Amen.

Prayers for Community
Discernment

Your congregation is participating in new justice work within the community

God, who never sleeps or slacks:

Each day, there are new, exciting opportunities for us to join you in your love and labor: crafting, cultivating, and cheering on your kingdom vision.

We give thanks, O God, that you share your kingdom vision with us.
You not only share your vision for kingdom, love, and labor with us:
You empower, equip, and embolden us as partners to imagine new possibilities for justice within our own community.
You invite us to love and serve alongside our neighbors as compassionate allies, committed advocates, and dear friends.
We have heard your call to serve as partners with you and our neighbors.
We have listened to our neighbors who have shared their needs, hopes, and ambitions.
And we have committed ourselves to new justice work within our community.

Gracious God, it is our holy and humble prayer that your way be revealed, your work be accomplished, and your will be done as we begin this new work within our community. Amen.

Your congregation is forming a new community partnership

God who is always doing a new thing,

We are grateful for the new thing you are creating in and through us here today. You have formed us not to do everything on our own but to be a part of your beloved community. We know that on our own, none of us can fully share your love, your justice, your compassion, and your peace. On our own we can only accomplish so much. However, when we come together as one community guided by your love and wisdom, God, then we are unstoppable.

So, we ask today that you bless this new partnership so that it may be for your good. May our work together help make our community more like your beloved community, a place where everyone is loved as they are and has what they need to thrive.

As we start this new relationship, help us to listen and learn from each other. Help us to support each other, to advocate for each other, and to be each other's best cheerleaders. When different strategies and opinions arise in how to do the work set before us, help us to always be curious instead of judgmental, and to assume the best in each other. When the work you have called us to is hard, help us to find times to seek your rest and joy in the midst of the work.

God we are so excited for this new partnership. We pray and we know that if we remain faithful to you that you will turn it into beautiful and powerful ministry that is better than anything that we could ever ask for or imagine. Amen.

Your congregation is considering a merger

Holy God, we know you are the God of each of us and the God of all of us. You have created each of us as unique individuals, and yet you call us to be in relationship with each other.

As this congregation contemplates their future, help us remember Jesus's prayer that "they may all be one" (John 17). May we live out that unity as we discern the potential of joining this body with another, allowing our two expressions of faith to meld into one. Give us vision to imagine new possibilities, temper our egos when we struggle to consider new dynamics, grant us patience and a listening heart when we have more questions.

As we mourn who we once were, may we see in this new relationship the possibilities of who we might be. Thank you, God, for calling each of us to be part of the larger body of Christ. May the refining fire of the Holy Spirit illuminate our path forward. Amen.

Your congregation is considering closing

O God of Wisdom,

You have shaped generations through this church.
You have nurtured our souls through worship, fellowship, and
　　service.
We praise you for this holy gift.

By the power of your Spirit open our minds and hearts.
Fill them with your wisdom as we contemplate closing this
　　church.
Help us to discern your will for our future.

Comfort us as we consider
the loss of this place of worship,
the loss of relationships,
the loss of this spiritual community

Encourage us to attend to sacred questions:
Who is God calling us to be?
What is God calling us to do?
Who is God calling us to serve?

Hold us, Resurrecting God, in your firm hands.
Keep us from being consumed with death.
Focus us on your promise of new life in Jesus Christ.

Amen.

Your congregation is considering significant changes to worship (time, format, etc.)

Steadfast Spirit, we give thanks for your enduring presence among us. We give thanks for the powerful ways you have spoken to us, as we gathered here to worship you. Move among us now, as we release our treasured traditions. Comfort us, as we grieve the loss of what has been. Rejoice with us, as we celebrate the blessings that have been poured out through this service.

Creator God, who breathes new life into all beings, let us trust this new thing you are doing through us now. Give us the courage to make a way in the wilderness where we have not gone before. Renew us, as we risk meeting you in new ways. Remind us that whenever, wherever, however we gather in your name, you are there.

May our worship be pleasing to you, O God, and draw us ever deeper into relationship with you. Amen.

Your congregation is considering becoming open and affirming

Into your wisdom, O Lord, we commit our spirits today. Reliant on your hope, trusting in your mercy, guided by your truth and compassion, we seek the journey your Spirit would have us take. Your word claims you are a lamp unto our feet, a light unto our path. You do not promise to shine a spotlight to the horizon, showing the destination immediately. And sometimes that makes us anxious.

Therefore, we pray that your peace surrounds this community, as we discern together whether our church should become Open and Affirming. We claim no clear endpoint at this outset. We simply pray for faith to see what next step your lamp shines unto our path, and for confidence, once we embark that direction, that you won't lead us astray.

For you are good, and you are love, and we aim in all things to be guided by those truths. And we long to make them also true of what we do, and who we welcome. We pray this by Jesus, our forever companion on the adventure of grace. Amen.

Your congregation is discerning ending a long-standing and historical program

Holy One, you are the one whom we are always serving and the one we devote our life to. We want you to know we celebrate and are thankful for the life-giving ministry all around us. May our prayer be a moment of thanksgiving for fellowship and unforgettable laughter. We will always reminisce the ways we saw the Holy Spirit working in this ministry and the ways that the ministry was important to so many people. We ask for your presence here as we practice faithful discipleship through discernment of our time, resources, and energy. Thinking about endings and change brings anxiety to our minds, and we already know that difficult conversations are ahead.

Give us the strength to face disappointment together and help heal the heartbreak that might be facing individuals who may not be ready to say goodbye. Be with us, God, as we spend time in sadness for what we miss, but help us to see a resurrection of ministry with what might come up. Scripture speaks of life after death; help us to be that energy to new life of your Church. Allow us to be brave enough to envision to new a life in Jesus that you might hold for us. Speak to us, lead us, and guide us in our work and beyond. Amen.

Your congregation is discerning adding a new staff position

Based upon Psalm 96

Singer of Our Songs,

You know the tunes of our hearts,
the rhythms of our days,
the echoing refrains of our hopes.

You know the melodies we have sung,
our orchestrations of baby blessings, weddings, baptisms,
funerals, projects, prayers, and so much good ministry

We have heard your call,
"Sing to the Lord, a New Song!"

With every voice, in the choir past,
to lyrists of today, we pray for the one
who will help us sing your song into the future.

In the cacophony of our chorus,
help us create space in our ranks.
Ring your tune, oh so clearly, in the ears of hearts.
So we might hear the one you gifted to lead us,
"Sing to the Lord, a New Song!"

In the anxious fluttering of our spirits,
blend our voices together in the calming breath of your Holy
Spirit.
So, we might bravely sing the song
your world needs to hear.

Together, as your Church,
"Sing to the Lord, a New Song!"

Your congregation is discerning becoming a bilingual worshiping community

*Please substitute the Spanish in this prayer for the language of your new bilingual context.

Holy One, you created a world in which your name is spoken, and your good news is shared in many different languages. We know you are a God of every voice and every language. We are grateful for your call to live and worship more fully into the diversity of your people, through this change, to be bilingual in our worship. Be with us as we grow, for we know change is hard.

Help us to offer grace and patience when this journey becomes a challenge. Help us be joyful. Fill us with *la paz y esperanza* for our future. For we know that your love does not have a primary language. *Levantemos nuestros corazones.* Let us pray that this new chapter in our worship helps bring the love and justice of God in a new way to our community. And may we grow together, seeing God anew in each other. *Demos gracias a Dios.* Thanks be to God. In your holy name we pray. Amen y Amén.

PRAYERS AND BLESSINGS FOR
COMMUNITY CELEBRATIONS

Your congregation is considering a building addition

God, we are grateful for your call to serve and for the story of Jesus to share. Bring wisdom to our journey toward a facility that enables our faithful service in this community. May reluctance for this new endeavor be met with patience. May fear of the unknown and potential risk be met with supportive Christian community. Raise our vision to see a future brightened by the potent ministry conducted in this space we seek to construct. We gratefully accept the tasks of stewardship and sacrifice to offer our resources toward your work in our midst, God. Use our dollars to build a building while we use our hearts, minds, and gifts to build your church in this place so that through this new space we might be a witness to your love and grace through Jesus. In the name of Christ, our cornerstone and foundation, Amen.

Your congregation is considering
a building remodel

Everything we have comes from you, God.
You've entrusted us with this world and all that's in it.

More than just walls,
you've given us a habitat for the holy.

Guide us now in our discernment,
that we might want what you want.

Give us eyes to see your vision for this place
and for us, your people.

Grant us a glimpse
into your holy imagination,
that we might look beyond ourselves.

Go with us, God,
into the future you have
for our space...
for your mission and ministry
through us...

Free us from our own limited imaginations
that we might become co-conspirators
in your creative mind,
extending through our vision,
your extravagant welcome for all. Amen.

Your congregation is seeding another congregation in your building

You have promised us, Holy One, that where two or three are gathered in your name, you too will be present. We give thanks for this promise, and we have felt its truth as we have gathered in this space to do the work of the church.

Now, a new community is preparing to step on to this holy ground. Bless this new congregation, God, as they gather together to hear your call for them, and to partner with you in the work you call them to.

Let your wisdom pour out of these walls, which have seen and heard much, and let your Spirit move in these spaces where they meet, just as it has for us, guiding them, inspiring them, and equipping them for the journey ahead.

Equip us to be good partners as well, as we mentor this new addition to the universal church. Let us be for them what you need us to be. We give thanks for the opportunity to witness and participate in the growth of the church. Amen.

Your congregation is supporting a new church start

God of new creation, we joyfully offer our prayers to this new opportunity for people to know you and be a part of your beloved community. We offer our fullest efforts and financial support to the formation of this new congregation. In conjunction with the faithfulness of these church planters, we commit to care for their work of sharing the Gospel of Jesus Christ.

Keep us ever grateful for those pioneering spirits whose generations-old strides gave rise to our own congregation. Root us in the story of God in this place that stretches to Peter and Paul and our call to make Christ known through community. Let our connection to our own congregation and our understanding of the early church give life to our support of this new church. May the body of Christ be strengthened in our support of this fresh mission to share the good news of Jesus to those who have yet to hear. Amen.

Your congregation is selling an existing building and relocating their ministry

Holy God, you who left behind heaven itself to become one of us in Jesus Christ, you know what it is to relocate for the sake of your people! Powerful God, you who are known to us now in the ever-portable Holy Spirit, you know what it is to give yourself fully wherever you are needed to be. Loving God, you who have held your people through the millennia surely hold this congregation now in the midst of transition, for you know what it is to transform your people.

As we let go of our familiar cocoon of this beloved building, we confess fear and sorrow as well as anticipation and trust. Help us to grow in courage and love for you and for one another. In our grief, we pray you will reshape us to be all you want this congregation to be. We ask that you fill us with your welcome for those we have yet to meet with whom we will share your love because we have moved with you. Help this congregation keep doing what is brave and wonderful and hard for the sake of your gospel. We believe you have opened a new chapter in the story of your faithfulness to us. We believe you are doing a new thing! And we know that you are the God who raises us up to new life, through Jesus Christ our Lord! Amen.

Your congregation is marking a first anniversary since something joyful

The psalmist instructs us to make a joyful noise to you, God, and today we lift up our voices of praise in such a way, in celebration of the great blessings we have experienced in you. Today we celebrate the one-year anniversary of a blessing and a joy to our community of faith (insert specific celebration).

We recall the experience itself, remembering the overwhelming feeling of your presence, as you celebrated alongside us in those moments. We give thanks for your presence then, now, and all the days in between, as you continue to guide us and celebrate each and every milestone with us.

We give thanks for the year since we first experienced this joy, because we have been inspired by it and carried it with us, using it as a motivation and brilliant memory, which continues to call us into relationship with each other, and with you.

We pray that you might continue to celebrate with us, O Great Inspiration, and bless our partnership with you, so that we have many more celebrations ahead. Amen.

Your congregation is sponsoring a family (immigrants, refugees, homeless transitioning)

Gracious and Loving Creator, we enter into a spirit of prayer to celebrate the opportunity to extend hospitality to the (insert name) family as they make a transition into their new life. We pray that we might offer our fullest support as we settle them into their future with joy and generosity of all our network of resources. We pray that through our kindness they might see your divine love, the love expressed through Jesus who charged us to love our neighbors.

We pray that the hopes and dreams that they have for their future unfold with your loving care surrounding them, God. That they meet the challenges of this new place and stage in life with the knowledge of the support of this community of faith that supports them.

We also pray for our community of faith that in sponsoring this family, that we might grow to understand more fully the neighbors Jesus calls us to love. As we grow in our knowledge of our neighbor, may we also grow in our love and our compassion, our sense of justice and mercy. Amen.

Your congregation is celebrating Pride Month

(For three or five or four leaders, and a full congregation. Can be adapted for a single voice prayer)

A voice cries out from the wilderness:

Make queer* the way of the Lord!

You, O Holy God, have created every person in your image—straight and bisexual, gay and lesbian, transgender, cisgender, agender, nonbinary, nonconforming, nonnormative, and the most vanilla among us.

You join us in our celebrations of the vital and blessed ways humanity is different. Renew us in our celebration of this spectrum of being that you created, bless, and call very good.

You, O Holy God, call us to remember.
That you are the God of Abraham, Isaac, and Jacob.
That you remembered the people of Israel as they groaned in slavery.
That you remembered the people when they strayed to other gods.
You, O Holy Christ, call us to remember.
That you are the bread of life, that yours is the cup of grace.
That you are the head, and we are the body.
Remember us to you—but not just us, and those like us.
Not just our stories and legacies, but the stories and legacies that do not
conform to our standards.
Not our will, but yours be done.

(Continued)

77

Remember us together into a greater Body, one that is complete only when all people know the length, breadth, width, and depth of your love, grace, and justice.

You, O Holy Spirit, call us to empowerment. From the beginning and to the end, you breathe life into the inert, you reflect light into the darkness, you give strength to the weary.

Release us from our biases; realize us in our community; reach us where we need stretching; breathe in us your new life.

You do not come quietly,
You come like a riot.
With tongues of flames on Pentecost
Like bricks through windows at Stonewall.
Unite us in your intentional peace, your wild freedom, your
    unstoppable joy.
Re-create in us that beautiful image of God.
Hear us now as we proclaim in the wilderness:
Make queer* the way of the Lord!

note from liturgist: "Queer" is a catch-all term adopted by many parts of the LGBTQ+ community, and when used without pejorative tone and intention of violence, it can be considered appropriate to name the nonheteronormative element. But, if your congregation would prefer a different word, "strange" or "bolder" could both work.

Your congregation is hosting worship prior to Pride Parade

Help us see people like you see them, Jesus.

Help us see the people who would never step foot in our church because they have been hurt, because they have been shunned, because they have been chased away by rules, doctrines, and orthodoxy. Help us be loving, inclusive, and reconciliatory.

Help us see the people who desperately need a faith community, who want to know they can still love you and worship you in a holy place, who have been waiting to be found and restored back into the fold. Help us be hospitable, inviting, and honest.

Help us see the people who cannot stomach a change in perspective, who have lists and placards ready to defend and decimate, who have all the answers and not many questions. Help us to not respond to evil with evil.

Help us see the people who are figuring out who they are in the fullness of how you created them, the people who are celebrating the radical difference you have called forth in them, and the people who are just there for the party. Help us share in the feast and celebrations.

Help us to see people the way you see people, Jesus Christ: as those worthy of and surrounded by God's love, as those sustained and maintained by the Holy Spirit, as those with gifts and graces that are so needed in this world. Amen.

Your community has received a significant economic benefit

Generous God,

You are the giver of all good gifts. All that we have is yours. and you call us to be stewards of what you have entrusted to us. We acknowledge this as we receive this wonderful gift. We are honored, and we are humbled that such generosity has been bestowed upon our community.

We are grateful for the generous heart of the giver. We ask that your love and grace continue to shine upon them. May they know what a blessing they have offered to us.

Help us now to discern your will. Empower us to be responsible stewards of this incredible gift. Give us the wisdom to use it faithfully.

Guide us to use it in the ways that will bring healing and wholeness to people's lives and to this community. Help us to use it in a way that will make the light of your love shine brighter.

May this gift call us to be equally generous with our treasure and with your grace. It's in your most holy name that we pray. Amen.

Your congregation experiences a significant spike in membership

We give you thanks, O God, for those who have recently entered into this community of faith. We pray that their time spent in the midst of this community is life giving and meaning making, as we journey together. Equip us, so we may be the Body you have called us all to be.

Give us open ears, so we may hear their stories, as well as their wisdom. Give us open eyes, so we may see the way you have worked in their lives, and identify the gifts you have given them. Give us open hearts, so we may love them as you created them.

We call upon your Spirit, Great Creator, that it might weave us together in deep relationship with one another, and with you. We also give thanks in this time for those who have long been committed to this congregation, for we have been witnesses to their work in creating a vibrant, welcoming space for all.

May we never stop seeking their wisdom, may we always honor their labor, knowing that they are called by you to do this work, and do it well they have. Amen.

Your congregation has received a significant gift

Generous God, we give you thanks and praise for this blessing which has recently been bestowed on our congregation. We acknowledge that you are the source of all gifts, and so we thank you for allowing this blessing to flow to our church. We bless the giver of this gift. We thank you for the generous spirit in which it was given.

Wise God, we now seek your counsel. We ask that you would lead us and guide us as we make decisions about how this gift will be used. Do not let our imaginations be limited, but help us dream big and get to work utilizing this gift so that others might come to know your love. Help us use this gift to serve your people, to care for the hurting, and reach out to those in need of hope.

We are your servants, o God, help us to use this gift to serve you better. With this gift and with all the blessings you give, may we realize these gifts are not ours, but yours. We ask that you would help us to be faithful, generous stewards of everything you have entrusted to us. May the fruits of our gifts be for your glory, now and forever. In the name of our greatest gift, Jesus Christ, we pray. Amen.

Your congregation has completed a successful capital campaign

God you are gracious and faithful. David once prayed, "Everything comes from you, and we have given you only what comes from your hand." Today, we celebrate our church's successful capital campaign completion as a living testimony of this ancient truth.

Thank you, God for the many gifts you allowed to pour into our church. Thank you for those who give sacrificially, let us use these gifts to honor that sacrifice. For those who give faithfully, let us use these gifts to glorify. For those who had nothing monetary to give but generously gave their prayers and encouragement, let us give thanks.

Now God, bless these gifts that with them we may do bountiful ministry that impacts lives and glorifies you.

Blessing for a Habitat for Humanity home

God who dwells with us,

You teach us to love our neighbors, so we know you rejoice with us, and with (insert name) family. As we bless this house built in love, we give thanks for the generosity of those who gave, so dreams of a good home could become reality.

We thank you for the willing hands that raised these walls; we thank you for the children who will grow up healthy and safe under this roof. We thank you for the strength you gave these parents, to hold their family together like liquid nails through hard times. We thank you for friends who will use this front door to come in and share meals and games, joys, and sorrows.

Wrap your arms around this home and family, like a great sheet of insulation, so they may always feel your protection and peace. Amen.

Your congregation is celebrating Earth Day

Holy Creator, you breathed into being the heavens and earth; you imagined the stars in the sky, the movement of the ocean from the moon, and it is so. Let us have the holy imagination to see all that has been spun into existence by your hand. On this Earth Day, give us eyes to see the awe and wonder of your world, O God, just as you imagined it.

God, forgive us when we fail to hold responsibly in our hands the gift you have entrusted us within your creation. Forgive us when we do not honor the life and breath and beauty of your creation, O God, and instead allow our death-dealing ways to destroy that which you have created by your hand. See our remorse, hear our repentance, and center our living on expressing our love for you through the way that we love what you have created. We pray that we might faithfully and creatively engage in the world around us as we pray in Christ Jesus. Amen.

Blessing for the demolishing of an existing building, with no plans to rebuild

God of every yesterday, today, and tomorrow, we offer our thanks, joy, and grief this day as we mark the passing of a building from our community's life.

We are grateful for the builders on whose shoulders we stand, for those that made space for our community to grow. We cherish the history of lives changed and service offered in our beloved space, and we bless new beginnings that came to be there.

We release to you our grief and sadness in this ending.

We give to you the anxiety and uncertainty that comes with this new beginning.

Empower us with your faithful Spirit so that we will embody the visionary strength of our ancestors and build an example for future generations.

Bless the dust of our building, and from it create within us the courage to face boldly our future together. Amen.

Prayers for Your Pastor

Your pastor calls in sick on Sunday

Healing God, we ask that you would surround our Pastor this day with your healing spirit. Sometimes we forget that pastors are human, that they experience joy and sorrow just like we do and that occasionally, they get sick. On this day of sabbath, allow (insert name) to rest and heal. Allow her/him to center on your love only and not be distracted by things left undone.

We, the church, are equipped to lead worship. You have put spiritual gifts within each one of us. Remind us that our words don't have to be perfect, but the intention of our hearts is what matters. Guide us with your Holy Spirit as we worship together this day.

The scripture says, "For where two or three are gather, there am I among them." (Matthew 18:20). We know that you are among us today, even though our Pastor cannot be. We are your children, and you will never leave us or forsake us.

Empower each of us to minister to one another as needs arise. Let us never, for one minute, think we need to be a professional to share the love of God. Call us to your service and give us the courage to answer the call. Strengthen us to be the body of Christ as we lead worship this day.

We thank you, God, for our Pastor whom we miss when he/she is gone. We thank you for this church and all the gifted people you have called to serve it. May we serve you without hesitation, this day and always. Amen.

Your pastor has been arrested in a nonviolent protest

Holy God, who calls each of us into the priesthood, we give thanks for the courageous leadership of our pastor and all who stood with them. Like many of the apostles who came before us, who penned their sacred stories, so we may better know God at work in the world, our church lifts up the bold leadership of our pastor and their peaceful stance against the injustices of your people.

We give thanks for this part of our story as a church. Lord, we also ask for the support of (insert pastor's name) while they are in the care of the state. May your justice lead the actions of the government, and your love prevail in righteousness for all people. Holy one, our church is thankful that Jesus lead the way before us, so that we may know that the emotions that accompany this time in the life of our church are held in your light and love. For you are the one who has paved the way and continue to light our path. In the holy name of Jesus, we pray. Amen.

Your pastor is about to lose their job and they don't know it

God of Grace, we give you thanks for creating us and calling us to be your body in this world. We celebrate your presence with us in the midst of our community of faith, even as we recognize that being a church family is a complex and sometimes difficult endeavor. We thank you for blessing us with the gift of relationship with each other, and we ask your forgiveness when those relationships don't always reflect your perfect love and mercy.

Loving God, as we prepare to enter into this important conversation, help us remember that we are all imperfect human beings who all fall short of your glory, and who are all redeemed, not by our own efforts, but by God's grace. We pray that our words are spoken and received with respect, and that everything we say and do is pleasing to you. We trust in your power to bring wholeness out of brokenness and turn endings into beginnings, and ask we you to illuminate our path forward. In Christ's name, Amen.

Your pastor is about to lose their job
and they know it

Ever changing, always present God—There are words we never
    imagined we would speak,
    decisions we never hoped to make,
    seasons we never sought to endure,
    yet still we find ourselves here.
In this moment of painful realization:
    the acknowledgement that clergy and congregation are
    not serving one another,
    the admission that it is time for a people and their pastor
    to part,
    the acceptance that moving forward together is no longer
    possible,
    remind us that you have walked this way before.
You do not fear death, but instead bless it with the promise of
    resurrection.
You do not avoid pain, but rather remind us that we are brave
    and courageous.
You call us to do hard things, to be bold, and speak the words
    that must be spoken.
There is sorrow in parting, grief in letting go,
    even doubt, in the decision to release.
May this work be done with your compassion and your grace,
    your honesty and your integrity,
    your faithfulness and your steadfast love,
    and, above all, may we remember that in beginnings and
    endings,
    new and old, hellos and goodbyes,
    we all remain your beloved children—
    bearers of your light and keepers of your peace.
Amen.

Your pastor has resigned suddenly out of conflict

Holy One,

Life in community is in the fabric of our faith—
    a messy and, at times, uneasy prospect.

When our hearts and minds fail to align
    with you and with one another,
    the threads we've woven together begin to fray.

Give us the courage to name our hurts,
    so that silence does not destroy us.

Where there is confusion,
    strengthen us with clarity.
Where there is sorrow,
    comfort us with compassion.
Where trust has been shattered,
    piece us together with perspective.

Heal the places within ourselves
    and this body
    that have been torn apart.
Reconcile us to you and to one another.
Reveal to us a path forward.
Restore in us hope for the future
    that we always have in you. Amen.

Your pastor is adopting a child

Holy and loving Parent, we are each your children and according to the scriptures you have given us "a spirit of adoption" rather than a spirit of fear. To be adopted means to be chosen, desired, and loved beyond biology. We thank you, O God, for loving each of us with this fierce kind of love.

Specifically today we pray for our pastor and (her/his/their) family. We love to watch the way you put families together and, God, we thank you that we have a front row seat to watch you knit this family together through adoption.

God, we acknowledge that there are so many unknowns in the process of adoption. Today we ask you to hold this family in the palm of your hand through all the scary parts of adoption. Be with them as they wait, show your favor to them through all the legal proceedings. Bind this family together, God, so that there would never be doubt that they belong together.

God of love, we know you bind up the brokenhearted and we are aware that there is brokenness in the adoption process as well. We ask you to hold this child (these children's) first (birth) family in your prayers as well. Heal the grief and bring comfort and peace into each life.

God, you have called our pastor into your service, but you have also called them to adopt. Acknowledging both of those callings, we ask that you would give us, the congregation, the patience to allow (her/him/them) to be a parent. We ask you to strengthen us to be the church for our pastor. May we love

(Continued)

one another well, and use our gifts to serve you, so that our pastor might have time and energy to love their family well. Help us as we support their new life together.

May this child (these children), now entering this family be our child(ren), just as (she/he/they are) is your child(ren). Like Hannah presented Samuel in the temple for dedication, we acknowledge that this child (these children) have been longed for and prayed for, and (she/he/they) belongs (belong) to you. We give you thanks for this answered prayer for our pastor and their family.

God, help each of us claim a spirit of adoption as we undergird this family with our love. We ask all these things in the name of our adopted brother, Jesus Christ. Amen.

Based on Romans 8:15-17 and 1 Samuel 1

Your pastor is beginning maternity leave

God of life, of love, of new beginnings, you have searched us and know us. You knit each of us together in our Mother's womb; we are marvelously made. We are in awe of the wonders of this miracle of life growing before us. Thank you for (insert name), for the ways she serves, loves, and leads us as we share in ministry together. Bless her and (partner/family) as they welcome their new baby and begin this incredible journey together.

May this time of leave be one of recovery, endless snuggles, and showering this little one with love. Bless our community during this time; that we might honor the space needed for this new family, sending them off with our prayers, love, support, and excitement for meeting little one when the time is right. Your love is woven through this community, and we delight in this joyful moment together. Amen.

Your pastor is beginning parental leave

God of New Life, we thank you that our pastor has welcomed a new child into (her/his/their) family and thereby into our community of faith. We thank you for the role of parent and what it teaches us about love, connection, dependency, and joy. Today our pastor steps away from their work with us to honor (her/his/their) call of parenting. We pray for them, for their family (name each member of the immediate family - partner and other children), that you guide them in the way of joy in exhaustion and peace in chaos. As this family learns a new rhythm, may they find it in you. As you knit this new creation together in their mother's womb, now God knits this family together in a new way.

And God we pray for our church. As we enter into a season without our pastor, open our eyes to new ways of serving and empower us to minister to one another. As we do so, allow us also to find joy in exhaustion and peace in the chaos. With joy, hope, gratitude, and a few nerves, we pray. Amen.

Your pastor is put on bed rest

With each day that passes, we wait,
O Holy One.

Every day, every hour, every minute,
a waiting and a wondering.
A gift, to be sure, and a struggle.

New life is a treasure,
We are filled with anticipation and joy for what might be.
As the new life you are bringing into this world grows,
We marvel at the miracle of your work.
As each day passes, every hour, every minute,
There is a strengthening, a growing, a becoming.

And yet, new life is fragile beyond imagining.
We are aware of this more than ever today,
As we wait and we pray and we hope,
And we cry and we ache and we worry.

Miracles are mixed with danger, every day.
We trust in the slow work of your Holy Spirit,
Your Creative, Healing Power at work within.

We pray, O God, for your presence to surround our pastor
As she holds all of this with you:
The anticipation and joy, the strengthening and growing,
As well as the fear and worry, the ache and the tears.

May we be courageous and unceasing in our prayers and
spacious presence

(Continued)

As we hold all of this with her:
The anticipation and hope, the stretching and growing,
The difficulty and disruption, the frustration and the sighs.

The waiting. With each day that passes, we wait, O Holy One,
Holding space for whatever you are bringing into our lives,
Whether heartache or joy, or a messy combination of all.

In the name of the Creator, Redeemer, and Sustainer of all life,
we pray. Amen.

Your pastor is placed on short-term medical leave

Holy Creator, we pray for our pastor (name) as they take leave from their work for a season of rest. We pray that you might work toward their fullest healing, giving them strength and patience in this necessary time. Allow their rhythm to slow so that their recovery might be elevated to its fullest pace. Give them the assurance they need to step away from this holy space and holy work to tend to their own body and spirit for a season.

These are anxious times as we temporarily shift how we lead your people in this place. God, we ask that you would assure us of your presence and wisdom that we might continue the work that has already been set into motion by your holy Spirit. Give us vision and insight to faithfully lead your church, God. Amen.

Your pastor has experienced the death of a child

God of the brokenhearted, our pastor and friend in faith is suffering the unfathomable grief of the death of (her/his/their) beloved child, (insert child's name). We pray with hope for your healing spirit to breathe life into *Pastor's family* as they live, always, with the heartache of this death. Let your healing touch extend to us also, for God this child was ours too.

We loved (child's name), we prayed for (her/him/them), and we claimed them as part of our church family. So, we ache alongside (pastor's name and family). And we pray that you would guide us as we tend to our pastor's grief and our own, remembering to leave space for the sharing of stories about our dear (child's name). Trusting in the new life you promise in Jesus, O God, we seek new life for (child's name) and for their family and church family. In the name of the risen one, we pray. Amen.

Your pastor's spouse/partner is diagnosed with an illness

God of Love, we give thanks for (spouse's/partner's name). (She/he/they) is a source of support and strength for (pastor's name) and their family, and now we humbly ask for support and strength for them. As Church, we lean on each other for encouragement and love and sometimes we forget the stresses and responsibilities of our Pastor and (her/his/their) family. We forget that they have lives and obligations outside of Church, that they have needs and challenges of their own. We thank you for all that they do to love and serve you and your people, and we ask for your blessing on them as they face this difficult time.

We ask that you surround them with your healing presence, that your Holy Spirit would anoint them with the blessing of your peace and love, and that you would guide our congregation to take up the responsibilities of leadership, teaching, and caring for one another so that their family may have time to heal and consider options for treatment. We ask your blessing on the doctors and nurses who care for them, that you would guide them and give them wisdom to provide the very best of care for (spouse's/partner's name). We ask that you would give (her/him/them) rest and patience throughout this time of healing.

We know that healing can take on many forms. Where we see suffering and fear, open our hearts to the possibility of new life. Where we see an end, help us to see a new beginning. Where we see death, help us to see the birth of love. We know that nothing can separate us from your love. We entrust (pastor's spouse/partner and pastor) and their family to your loving care. We thank you for their ministry together and we pray that your love would carry them through this time.

We ask these things in Jesus' name. Amen.

Your pastor's spouse/partner passes away unexpectedly

Intercede with deep sighs, God, in these painful moments where we simply do not know how to pray as we ought. Allow us to enter in the enveloping arms of your Spirit's care. Accept the brokenness of this congregation, which is shaken by the loss of our pastor's beloved (wife/husband/partner), (name).

Keep us mindful that our collective grief is the aggregate of individual journeys. Weave tenderness and awareness into our interactions in this season of loss. Help us seek appropriate expectations of ourselves, of one another. and especially of our pastor in (her/his/their) extraordinary sorrow. Use each of us to proclaim to one another the gospel that promises comfort now and joy eternal. May we rest ourselves in these truths of Jesus. Amen.

Your pastor is diagnosed with a life-threatening illness

God who created (pastor's name), who knit them together in their mother's womb, who passed (her/him/them) through the waters of baptism and called them to a life of service in Jesus' name, thank you for our pastor. Thank you for holding (her/him/them) through these days of receiving and adjusting to frightening news about their health.

O Good One, we hold (pastor's name) in the light of your healing for (her/his/their) body, mind, and spirit. We pray for every resource needed for them to be made whole again to be marshalled at their side. We trust that you are at work in ways we cannot see to bring all things together for them good. We ask that you give (pastor's name) a new testimony of your goodness, mercy, and power. Please help our congregation know how to be partners in (her/his/their) healing as we continue in ministry together. Let us build each other up in the journey ahead, so the world may know that this is how Christians love, and this is who you are. Amen.

Your pastor has died suddenly

God of all life, we trust in your promises of goodness and mercy, and yet we struggle to feel your presence in the face of such a tragic loss. We are now sheep without a shepherd. But we know Jesus is the Good Shepherd, and that he will guide us through this darkest valley.

We give you thanks for the leadership of (pastor's name), who showed us through (her/his/their) ministry what it meant to depend on you in the face of life's challenges. We now seek to live out what we have learned from (her/him/them) as we deal with their death. We pray that (she/he/they) has now inherited the promises about which they so lovingly taught us. We don't understand, God, but we trust in you to guide us. Receive your servant (pastor's name) and comfort those of us who will miss them so dearly. Amen.

A beloved former pastor dies suddenly

Loving God, in the Great Commission, Jesus calls for us to go out and make disciples, and today we honor someone who lived out to that call. We thank you for (representative's name) ministry and for the ministry of this beloved pastor (pastor's name) that had a great impact on all our lives. We remember the time of sharing in prayer where we were better connected to you because of (her/his/their) spoken words and silent thoughts. We recall the life-changing milestones where our pastor stood beside us, knowing that you were working through (her/him/them) so that we might feel your presence. May this attitude of a true servant leader inspire us to live out another calling to the Church. We pray for the future and for the unity of our church family feeling the loss of someone dear, and that you provide a comforting Spirit when we find ourselves in the midst of undeniable grief. Holy one, we have a better vision of love because we have known this person, and we ask for your continual and sustaining strength so that we may live out the love that Christ taught us. Amen.

Your pastor is divorcing

Loving God,
Your people know there is a season for all things-
a time to live and a time to die,
a time to sow and a time to reap,
a time to rejoice and a time to mourn.

On this day, loving God, we mourn.
We mourn the loss of a relationship and a life together.
We mourn because of the pain of heartbreak and the separation
    that comes when a marriage ends.
We mourn because of the pain of our pastor and the feast of
    losses she endures.

And, on this day, loving God, we also rejoice.
We rejoice in the courage required to acknowledge an ending.
We rejoice in the boldness demonstrated by those who do not
    fear the loss of a dear thing.
We rejoice in the strength of our clergy who has modeled the
    path of death and resurrection, pain, and new life.

May we as a congregation offer support when it is needed with
    voices, hands, and hearts.
May we sense the time for silence and the time for speech,
the time for space and the time for surrounding her with grace,
the time to mourn and the time to weep.

Above all, may we witness to the mystery,
the new life,
the resurrection,
that continues to unfold in our midst.

Thanks be to God.
Amen.

Your pastor is facing criminal charges

God, we are so very human. We know that each of us is made in your image and that we are all doing our imperfect best to love and serve you. And yet, our hearts are broken at the news of hearing that (pastor's name) has broken the law. We are disappointed, angry, and confused. Trust has been lost and doubts arise. Our faith is shaken. How can this happen, God?

Still - how can we be surprised, when scripture is full of stories of faithful people who broke covenant and failed to keep holy promises? We all fall short of your grace. And yet, your love remains. Thank you for loving us for who we are. Thank you for receiving the very worst and forgiving us.

Help us to find a way through this. What does forgiveness look like? We cannot forget what has happened. We may never trust (pastor's name) the same way again, but we still love them and that's why this hurts. That's why we are angry. Receive this anger, God, and help us to overcome it. Help us to live, not as victims, but as lovers. Love is difficult sometimes, God. It is illogical. It is hard. Sometimes it feels as though it might destroy us.

Yet we know that the merciful are blessed because they have had mercy shown to them. Show us mercy, Holy God, that we may show it to (pastor's name). Help us to know salvation through forgiveness. This does not mean love without consequence. This is not the same as pretending this didn't happen. We can't do that. We prayerfully surrender (pastor's name) to you. Help us to discern the way forward. Give us wisdom, God.

(Continued)

Pruning is also biblical. If it is time to release (pastor's name) from (her/his/their) call, please help us to do so lovingly and in a way that honors the lives of everyone who has been impacted by this breaking of covenant. By your grace and holy imagination, restore us to wholeness.

In Jesus' Name, Amen.

Your pastor has been accused of sexual misconduct

God of us all,

We must hold and confess in your light and love, news that feels dark and difficult:

Our pastor has been accused of sexual misconduct.

And we are struggling with the news, O God.

Our spirits are uneasy.

How will we navigate the days and weeks ahead, filled with searching questions and bruised hearts?

Our minds are racing.

How can we care for everyone who is impacted by these allegations, within and beyond our community of faith?

Our hearts are heavy.

How will our congregation ever feel healthy and whole again when relationships are strained and trust is broken?

We speak aloud this difficult reality, not yet knowing the path or process forward for resolution. We admit our own woundedness and wondering as we hear this news. And we ask questions of you, God (and of one another), yearning to see the path forward.

Today, O God, help us remember that in dark and difficult times, you are with us—breathing new breath into our very being, listening to our questions, and leading us forward in discernment as faithful servants of your beloved community. Amen.

Your pastor has been caught in an embarrassing situation

God of Mercy,

We seek you now for one that serves you is in trouble. Our pastor, a leader in our church, and their family need you.

We approach gently because we too have been in trouble. Help us to balance care and accountability, responsibility, and restoration.

Help us to guard our mouths from gossip or slander, but also speak the truth in love. Help our church access and maintain healthy boundaries to protect us and our leaders.

As you sent your people in the past, send us a Deborah—or Jethro—with wise, seasoned counsel for those who deeply care for our leader and our community.

God of Mercy,

Hear our prayer.

Your pastor is deployed as a chaplain

Great God of my heart,

You who see what I cannot see,
You who are present where I cannot be present.

I trust in your peace;
I live within your hope,
But even still I feel overwhelmed during my time of prayers:

Our beloved pastor ministers in a place void of peace and hope, a land of war.

There is so much we don't know;
The silence paints our imagination with fear;
Time does not allay our angst or lessen the danger.

Give me the courage to love the family left behind;
Provide me the strength to care for the church struggling with the same;
Show me how to be present to both within your grace.

Teach me how to rise above myself in this moment.

Fill me with patience for her eventual return;
Lessen the anxiety that this war will change our minister;
Create a bridge of peace to bind our hearts anew.

My soul is like a psalm,
I cry, "Bring her home safe."

God speed, servant of the Lord, God speed. Amen.

Pastor is transitioning to a new role within the ministry

God, we gather in joyous celebration as we transition (pastor's name) to their new calling within our congregation. We give thanks for the faithful work that they have already sewn into your ministry at (congregation's name) as they served as (insert previous role). Continue that good and faithful work in our community, God and help us to build a bridge to this new calling we have placed on (pastor's name). Continue in them as well as in this church a continued heart for you, God, and a heart for your people.

Ground this specific calling in the larger calling of your work in the world, O God. Remind each of us of how you call us and how you change us in the process. Allow each of us gathered here to support (pastor's name) in their new role, while we each renew our calling to share your good news of the love you have for us in Christ Jesus. Amen.

Blessings for a pastor departing for sabbatical

Holy One of Rest and Renewal,

You are the source of all that is good, holy, and peaceful. You created us to be in full covenant with you with body, mind, and spirit. In these moments we acknowledge that pastoral ministry is both demanding and rewarding. We give pause as we pray intentionally to give blessing and peace to our minister of the Gospel (pastor's name) that (she/he/they) will find the needed time and space for a renewed soul, a refreshed spirit, an energized mind, and a cared-for body.

We pray (she/he/they) will create needed space for openness to God's leading. May there be time to faithfully attend to the soul. May there be time to find joy with family. May there be time to play and simply be with God, others, and self.

We pray that (pastor's name) will find helpful ways to disconnect with the church in healthy ways so as not to be so worried or consumed with what is going on with the church in their absence. Let them trust God and the church leaders to faithfully care for all that will need attention and compassion in the time away.

(Continued)

We know, O God, that Sabbath is not vacation but intentional time to deepen one's love for God and for what God loves. May our minister be open to receiving from God's presence and strength, which will guide, support, encourage, and surround (her/him/them). Let space be made for play, rest, thoughtfulness, and dreaming.

We offer this prayer of blessing upon our minister because we have been truly blessed by them and support and love them in this time of revitalization.

We pray in the name of Jesus, who always seemed to know that people needed the most in that moment. We pray that the powerful ministry of Jesus will speak a word of hope and healing to our minister as they now find a new rhythm for ministry, for their life, for their walk with God.

All this we pray in the name of the one who claims us and loves us, Jesus the Christ. Amen.

Blessing for a pastor returning from sabbatical

It is with joy that we welcome (pastor's name) back from (her/his/their) sabbatical, and offer this blessing on his/her leadership among us.

We know that "in six days the LORD made the heavens and the earth, and on the seventh day he rested and was refreshed." And so we pray that you, our Creator God, will sustain a spirit of renewal in (pastor's name) as they steps back into their role here at (church's name). May the flame of excitement ignited as they explored new ideas and places continue to guide them in their work, so that their passion for your service burns strong.

May your light, O Lord, be kindled in each of us, that we may be a beacon of hope for you. Teach us all when to join in your creative work, and when to rest and seek the refreshment only you can give. Amen.

ABOUT THE CONTRIBUTORS

Rev. Robyn Bles is the Senior Minister at Wakonda Christian Church in Des Moines, Iowa; she finds deep satisfaction and joy in spending time with her partner and daughter and in running. Bles wrote the prayer on page 67.

A Senior Pastor, a Brigade Chaplain, a husband, father, and combat veteran, Rev. Owen Chandler lives by the mantra that "love matters most" and weaves this hope within all that he does, says, and creates. Chandler wrote the prayers on pages 9 and 111.

Rev. Whitney Waller Cole is the Senior Minister at Creekwood Christian Church, Flower Mound, Texas, whose faith in God and humanity is renewed everyday by the movement of the Spirit, the daily practice of resurrection, and the songs of The Hold Steady. Cole wrote the prayers on pages 60 and 109.

Rev. Audrey Connor is a graduate of Vanderbilt Divinity School and is currently teaching math in Columbus, Ohio. Connor wrote the prayer on page 34.

Rev. Melanie Harrell Delaney is the Lead Pastor of Good Shepherd Christian Church in Macedonia, Ohio, the Communications Coordinator for Bethany Fellows, and mom to Owen, Olivia, and Clayton. She is married to Rev. Tyler Delaney, a hospice chaplain for the Cleveland Clinic. Delaney wrote the prayer on page 97.

Rev. Diane Faires serves as Senior Minister of St. Paul's Christian Church in Raleigh, NC, where she enjoys hiking, running, and volunteering with Habitat for Humanity. Faires wrote the prayers on pages 19, 23, 25, 64, 84, and 115.

Rev. Shauna St. Clair Flemming, MDiv, MPH, is a graduate of Vanderbilt Divinity School and an ordained minister at Ray of Hope Christian Church (DOC). Flemming wrote the prayer on page 83.

Rev. Kara K. Foster is the Senior Minister of First Christian Church (Disciples of Christ) in Madisonville, Kentucky. The joy of her life is her husband, Mark, and her children, Annie and Luke. Foster wrote the prayer on page 49.

Rev. Cara Gilger is an author, artist, and minister who has served churches in Texas, Tennessee, and Indiana for over 15 years; she lives with her partner, their two daughters, and their dog in the Dallas area. Gilger wrote the prayers on pages 21, 32, 35, 43, 76, 85, 99, and 112.

Rev. Danny Gulden serves the church as a Vice President with Pension Fund of the Christian Church. He blogs at therevdanny. com. Gulden wrote the prayers on pages 48 and 80.

Rev. Jamie Lynn Haskins is ordained in the Christian Church (Disciples of Christ) and serves as the Chaplain for Spiritual Life at the University of Richmond in Richmond, Virginia. Haskins wrote the prayers on pages 12, 91, and 106.

Rev. Megan Houston is the Senior Minister at First Christian Church, Bowling Green, Kentucky; where she has merged her passion for justice and sustainability in her work with the Poor People's Campaign and the farm she shares with her partner and twin daughters. Houston wrote the prayer on page 6.

Rev. Shane Isner is the husband of Rev. Tabitha Isner, father of Tymari Isner, and Senior Minister of First Christian Church (Disciples of Christ) of Montgomery, Alabama. Isner wrote the prayers on pages 29, 37, and 65.

Rev. Stephanie Kendell is the Executive Minister of Park Avenue Christian Church in New York City, where she enjoys building community through the arts, and seeking equity and justice for all God's people. Kendell wrote the prayers on pages 17, 44, 45, 68, and 89.

Rev. Billy Doidge Kilgore is an ordained minister in the Christian Church (Disciples of Christ) and lives with his wife and two sons in Nashville, Tennessee. Kilgore wrote the prayers on pages 54 and 63.

Rev. Elizabeth King prays and writes out of her experience as Minister of Congregational Care at Central Christian Church in Lexington, Kentucky, as mom to a compassionate and creative boy, and as a seeker of spiritual wisdom and practice. King wrote the prayers on pages 26, 39, and 100.

Rev. Sarah Kingsbury lives into God's call to love, serve, and worship as the Associate Minister at First Christian Church (Disciples of Christ) in Jefferson City, Missouri. Kingsbury wrote the prayer on page 15.

Rev. Allison Lanza serves as the Associate Minister at Ridglea Christian Church in Fort Worth, Texas and founder and director of Connect Fort Worth, a mission site that empowers groups to put their faith into action in their own communities through service and justice in ways that are relational, sustainable, and dignity-giving. Lanza wrote the prayers on pages 50 and 61.

Rev. Kyle McDougall is the Associate Minister at First Christian Church (Disciples of Christ) in Bowling Green, Kentucky and a Bethany Fellows alum. McDougall wrote the prayers on pages 10 and 51.

Rev. Peter Mitchell is a husband and father, a two-time grad of Texas Christian University; he drinks lots of coffee, loves the lake. and is pastor of Marion Christian Church in Marion, Iowa. Mitchell wrote the prayers on pages 70, 73, and 102.

Rev. Amanda Hatfield Moore serves as the pastor of Hillsville Christian Church in Hillsville, Virginia. Moore wrote the prayers on pages 11, 13, and 58.

Rev. Ryan Motter serves as the Associate Minister at Community Christian Church in Kansas City, Missouri, and is the co-creator of the podcast "My Pastor Friend Says." Motter wrote the prayers on pages 36 and 86.

Rev. Suzanne Motter serves as the Minister for Children and Families at Community Christian Church in Kansas City, Missouri, while soaking up the joy and laughter of raising two daughters with her partner, Ryan. Motter wrote the prayer on page 95.

Rev. Amy Piatt is the Minister of Mission and Family Life at First Christian Church, Grandbury, Texas, where she cohosts the Homebrewed Christianity podcast with her husband, Christian Piatt, and co-parents Mattias and Zoe. Piatt wrote the prayers on pages 101 and 107.

Rev. Jamie Plunkett is a graduate of Texas Christian University and Brite Divinity School who serves as Minister of Youth and Families at University Christian Church in Fort Worth, Texas, and is an avid Horned Frog sports fan. Plunkett wrote the prayers on pages 72, 75, and 81.

Rev. Joey Pusateri, pastor of First Christian Church in Danville, Kentucky, is a father, husband, and disciple of Jesus who believes that hope is the birthright of every human being. Pusateri wrote the prayers on pages 8, 20, and 30.

Rev. Antonio Redd is a husband, father, son, brother, and friend who loves building a community of people who loves God and the call to justice. Redd wrote the prayers on pages 31, 46, and 57.

Rev. Sunny Ridings is the Senior Minister at First Christian Church, Rockwood, Tennessee, where she practices loving God and loving people, especially her partner and son. Ridings wrote the prayers on pages 82, 88, and 93.

Rev. Kim Gage Ryan is the Director of the mentoring ministry Bethany Fellowships, following 27 years in congregational ministry. Ryan wrote the prayer on page 52.

Rev. Melissa St. Clair is the Senior Minister at Heart of the Rockies Christian Church (Disciples of Christ) in Fort Collins, CO, where she prays and plays on the nearby trails and mountains. St. Clair wrote the prayers on pages 53, 71, and 92.

Rev. Shanna Steitz the Senior Minister of Community Christian Church in Kansas City, Missouri, co-creator of the podcast "My Pastor Friend Says" and serves on the board for the Bethany Fellowships. Steitz wrote the prayer on page 86.

Rev. Arthur Stewart is Senior Minister of Midway Hills Christian Church, where he leads with a strong commitment to justice and a knack for quirky church marquee signs. Stewart wrote the prayers on pages 22, 41, 77, and 79.

Rev. Casey Tanguay is the Minister to Families and Professionals at First Christian Church in Garland, TX, and an Oncology Certified Registered Nurse at UT Southwestern Medical Center. Tanguay wrote the prayer on page 16.

Rev. Dr. Dawn Darwin Weaks is pastor to Connection Christian Church in Odessa, Texas; partner to husband Joe; parent to teens Arwen and Sam; and through it all, pray-er to God, who saves her every day. Weaks wrote the prayers on pages 74 and 103.

Rev. Kory Wilcoxson serves as Senior Minister at Crestwood Christian Church in Lexington, Kentucky, where he spends time with his family and rooting for the Kentucky Wildcats. Wilcoxson wrote the prayers on pages 62, 90, and 104.

Rev. Dr. Christopher Wilson is the senior minister of Rush Creek Christian Church in Arlington, Texas and currently serves as the board chair for Bethany Fellowships. Wilson wrote the prayers on pages 7, 27, and 113.

Rev. Mark Winters loves his family, tells bad jokes, tries to go bicycling when he can, and really enjoys being the pastor of First Congregational United Church of Christ in Naperville, Illinois. Winter wrote the prayer on page 40.

Rev. Dietra Wise is a preacher, organizer, and trainer who lives with her family in St. Louis, Missouri. Wise wrote the prayers on pages 56 and 110.

Rev. Katherine Wright is the Minister of Family Life and Community at Central Christian Church (Disciples of Christ) in San Antonio, Texas, and is a Disciple Fellow of Bethany Fellows. Wright wrote the prayers on pages 47, 66, and 105.

Rev. Selena Wright is the Pastor of Kirk of Bonnie Brae United Church of Christ in Denver, Colorado, mother of three girls, and a person of faith who always prays with her eyes open, for God is always in view. Wright wrote the prayers on pages 14, 24, 33, 38, 55, and 96.

ABOUT BETHANY FELLOWSHIPS

Since 1999 Bethany Fellowships has been encouraging young pastors in their earliest years of ministry. This ministry was born out of the intention of strengthening congregations of the Christian Church (Disciples of Christ) by helping newly ordained, young pastors transition from seminary to sustained congregational ministry with a strong and healthy pastoral identity. Research indicated one third of young ministers might leave congregational ministry in their first five years. The good news is that Bethany Fellowships is helping to change that reality for Disciples pastors and congregations.

In the fall of 2014 a Bethany Fellows Ecumenical group launched with the same mission to a wider group of young ministers, from a variety of denominations. Today Bethany Fellowships celebrates the Disciples Bethany Fellows, Ecumenical Bethany Fellows as well as having encouraged a similar ministry for those engaged in campus ministry and college chaplaincy.

The Bethany Fellowships ministry model provides four years of support and encouragement by offering two retreats each year and helping young pastors develop a rhythm of spiritual practices and patterns for a lifetime of ministry. While on retreat the Fellows receive the prayerful support of experienced pastors/mentors and the encouragement of significant collegial relationships. The retreat also includes a visit with dynamic congregations and leaders, fueling creativity and insights to share with the Fellows' congregations. Through Bethany Fellowships young ministers are better able to navigate the beginnings of a pastoral vocation, as well as crucial young adult life transitions, building confidence and strengthening leadership.

Bethany Fellowships is also in partnership with the Pension Fund of the Christian Church, facilitating the peer group component of the Pension Fund's Excellence in Ministry program. The Excellence in Ministry pilot program seeks to reduce or alleviate some of the key financial pressures that inhibit effective pastoral leadership of early career ministers, and improve the financial literacy and management of leaders and their congregations through education.

More information can be found at bethanyfellows.org or by contacting Rev. Kim Gage Ryan, Director, 573.489.2729

Printed and bound by PG in the USA